A TEACHER'S GUIDE TO

USING ABBEYS

Cynthia Cooksey

English ✷ Heritage

CONTENTS

ENGLISH HERITAGE

**Capital, St Augustine's
Abbey, Kent**

Nuns at prayer

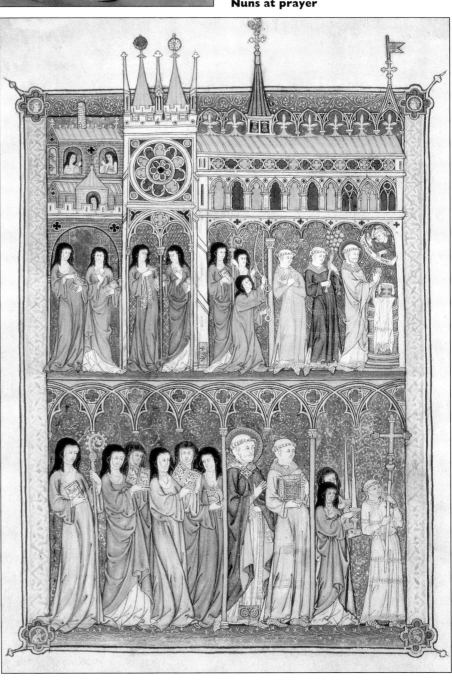

BRITISH LIBRARY

ABOUT THIS BOOK

Compare these two photographs. They highlight the challenge in choosing abbeys as a teaching resource - how to enable a pupil, faced with puzzling ruins, to see the complete abbey in the mind's eye. This handbook aims to meet that challenge and to show you how to use the primary evidence of the site itself to explain the nature of the lives that were lived there.

Sitework offers the chance to focus in depth on historical studies or range out more widely across the curriculum. Children can develop skills in observation, deduction, analysis and hypothesis. In follow-up work they can test their hypotheses against evidence from other sources - just the type of rigour advocated in the National Curriculum. All of these aspects are covered in this book. The immediate focus may seem narrow but abbeys perfectly exemplify the importance of religion in the Middle Ages, a key concept in an understanding of the period.

A close look at abbeys brings out significant parallels with today - the need for rules to maintain social order, the obligation to care for the poor, aged and infirm and the dangers of over-concern with material values. Consideration of such issues forces children to argue from first principles rather than unthinkingly accept familiar solutions.

ENGLISH HERITAGE

Castle Acre Priory, Norfolk

ENGLISH HERITAGE

Artist's impression by Alan Sorrell of Castle Acre Priory, Norfolk

HISTORICAL BACKGROUND

ORIGINS

The need to get away from it all and find spiritual peace drove the early hermits to choose solitary lives. But seeing the advantage in numbers, some began to group together in the Near Eastern deserts in the late fourth century AD and so begin the development of Christian monasticism. Gradually the practice spread even to the remote western fringes of the British Isles, such as Northern Ireland, where men of the Celtic church spent their lives in individual cells which stood alone or clustered together.

St Benedict's Rule

The most significant code of observance for such communal living was originated by St Benedict in Italy. He wrote his 'Little Rule For Beginners' in the early sixth century for a community who were mostly laymen like himself, for it was not the norm for a monk to be a priest until the later Middle Ages. His monks

house was autonomous, united to its fellows only in a loose federation and in obedience to the Rule. The larger houses, ruled by an abbot or abbess, became known as abbeys; the lesser ones - daughter cells ruled by a prior responsible to the abbot of the mother house - were called priories. The term convent was used equally for houses of monks or nuns. A life of poverty and chastity was implicit in acceptance of the Rule. The monks' day, except for Sunday which was devoted entirely to worship, was divided into three parts :

- the hours of prayer and worship
- the hours of study
- the hours of work (manual labour)

By the tenth century the emphasis on manual labour had largely been dropped. The Benedictines became renowned not only for their magnificent architecture but also for their splendid services, illuminated manuscripts and scholarship.

the first Benedictine monastery at Canterbury and his followers spread Christianity northwards.

From Iona, off the west coast of Scotland, had come a different, Celtic strain of monasticism based on the tradition of the early desert communities. It inspired Aidan to make his monastery at Lindisfarne a major training centre for missionaries who then founded other abbeys along the coast.

GLORY, DISASTER AND REBIRTH

From Lindisfarne a succession of missionaries pushed south to promote the Celtic variant of Christianity whilst from Canterbury others moved north to spread the Roman tradition of the Benedictines. Eventually the latter version became accepted practice. There followed a golden age of art, architecture and learning, but it did not last - the Viking raids of the eighth and ninth centuries almost entirely obliterated Anglo-Saxon monasticism. Not until the

BRITISH LIBRARY

St Benedict of Monte Cassino, c480-c550, the **founding father of western monasticism**

BODLEIAN LIBRARY, OXFORD

Benedictine monk professing to his abbot

lived together communally in his monastery at Monte Cassino. His Rule was so balanced and moderate that it gained wide acceptance in other monasteries. Each Benedictine

Founding fathers

The Rule was brought to England in AD597 by St Augustine, an Italian monk sent by Pope Gregory the Great to convert the English. He founded

late tenth century when Archbishop Dunstan, himself a monk, led the revival of monasticism were religious manuscripts, metalwork, and ivories of the highest quality again produced.

Cluny

An offshoot of the Benedictines had originated at Cluny in Burgundy c.910. The Cluniacs followed the Rule, but developed a far more elaborate ceremonial including the use of rich vestments, lavish architectural designs and sumptuous decoration. New foundations remained as dependent priories under the control of the mother church of Cluny herself.

Cluniac Priory, Castle Acre, Norfolk

Norman expansion

By 1087, when William the Conqueror died almost all the existing abbots had been replaced by Normans. In a massive building programme earlier houses were rebuilt in stone and new ones were sited at or near growing centres of population or long-hallowed shrines. The number of monks and nuns swelled, libraries and schools expanded and the liturgy (form of church service) and chant (type of church music in which prose is sung) were revitalised. In some of the most important monasteries, like Canterbury and Winchester, the monastic churches became cathedrals. Here the bishop replaced the abbot and the prior ran the community's everyday affairs.

REFORM

With rising importance and wealth came a falling-away from original ideals of poverty, asceticism and purity. Occasionally, attempts at reform ended in a breakaway movement to establish a new order with a more stringent code.

The Cistercians

The Cistercian Order arose in 1098 at Cîteaux, in Burgundy, in an effort to set new standards and high ideals. Distracting decoration in church architecture, vestments and plate was forbidden and elaboration of ritual and chant rejected. Food was simple and the habit made of unbleached, undyed wool - hence the name White Monks. Sites were to be sought in remote places, never in towns or cities. Only one room was to have a fire, the brethren were to sleep on bare boards and labour daily in the gardens rather than study in the cloister. The ideal was to return to self-sufficiency by a denial of the feudal income which other orders relied upon and a refusal to make money out of holy relics or public appeals. Gifts of land would be accepted and farmed by a new class of monk, the 'conversi' or lay brothers, who took a lesser version of the monastic vows, remained uneducated and spent only two brief periods daily in church. The centralised order spread rapidly, independent of feudal power. With pioneering zeal, the Cistercians cleared and drained remote areas of northern England, Scotland and Wales and some abbeys grew extremely wealthy from agriculture, cattle and horse breeding and, especially, wool production.

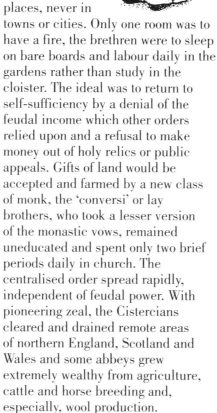

The Carthusians

The Carthusian Order, founded in 1084 in the French Alps and restricted to men only, was even more austere. Each monk slept, ate,

worked, prayed and recited the holy offices in his separate quarters, remaining in seclusion except at occasional communal gatherings and at services. There were few such Charterhouses in England and Wales and the only substantial remains are at Mount Grace in Yorkshire.

The Augustinians

The Augustinian Order, which used a fairly short and adaptable Rule based on that of St Augustine of Hippo, reached England probably in 1104. It was unique in that the brethren, known as Black Canons, were all priests who might work outside the cloister, taking daily services in parish churches. They ran schools, hospitals and almshouses, and quickly became popular and influential.

The Gilbertines

There was only one specifically English order - the Gilbertines, who revived the double-community of monks and nuns of Celtic monasticism. The sexes shared a common church, subdivided by a high central wall so that they could hear but not see each other.

Nuns

Nunneries fared badly after the Viking raids, never regaining their former status and influence. Compared with monasteries, most had smaller premises, less money, poorer libraries and a lower standard of education.

ENGLISH HERITAGE

5

Friars

The friars, who arrived in England in the early thirteenth century, were very different from the monks since they settled among the people, in friaries built for them by benefactors. They owned nothing and existed on alms and charity. They preached in the native tongue in streets and market places as well as in parish churches, tended the poor and sick, and studied and taught. At first they were popular but lost favour when they lapsed from their earlier humility. The four main orders were the Franciscans (Grey Friars), Dominicans (Black Friars), Carmelites (White Friars) and Augustinians (Austin or White Friars).

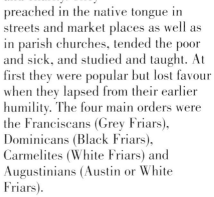

GROWTH

In the twelfth century the number of English and Welsh monasteries quadrupled. In the thirteenth century the rise continued more slowly, by the middle of the fourteenth century expansion had peaked and thereafter there were hardly any new foundations. At the peak there were just over 1000 religious houses in England and Wales with an average of around seventeen persons under vow in each house. With a total national population of approximately 4,000,000, some 10% to 15% of the country's wealth was controlled by less than 1% -those who had taken the vow - and almost all of that control was concentrated in the hands of the top forty or fifty people.

Abbot's lodging, Muchelney Abbey, Somerset

Wealth

Monasteries had become inescapably wealthy through the ownership of land. Rich patrons endowed them with ever more estates, including manors and villages, in the hope of dividends in the world to come. The income this created - produce in land, and labour dues and rents - then passed to the abbey. Similarly the gift of the patronage of a church brought an income from its fees, tithes and glebe land, less the amount needed to maintain the priest. Additional cash flowed in as offerings from pilgrims, dues from markets held outside the precincts and profits from monastic mills.

Detail of postmill, Rievaulx Abbey, North Yorkshire

Tithe barn, Bradford-on-Avon, Wiltshire

Monk shearing sheep

CHANGES

With the growth of a money economy, villeins paid their dues in money rather than in service, so abbeys had to hire their labour force. In the thirteenth century, aiming at greater efficiency, they began to exchange parcels of land to consolidate their estates and turned to large-scale sheep farming or grain production. However, by the early fourteenth century some abbeys, gambling on wool prices, had sunk desperately into debt. Then came disaster.

The Black Death

Of the population at large, about 30% died of the plague in 1348-49: in the abbeys it was over 50%, reducing the numbers of those under vow from 17,000 to 8,000. With the diminished labour supply, more abbeys rented out land to direct tenants or turned to wool production, thus accelerating existing economic trends. So the monasteries clung on to what was an increasingly disproportionate share of the country's land and wealth whilst their inhabitants slowly dwindled in number - an imbalance which provoked bitter feelings outside.

Status

By the fifteenth and sixteenth centuries the mere fact of landownership had long forced abbots and priors out of the cloister and into the world, where they were inevitably involved in problems of management, administration, justice and marketing. In the larger houses the abbots had the responsibilities of great feudal lords. Five abbesses ranked as baronesses and thirty abbots as barons with seats in the House of Lords. Able and educated, they were used by the government as versatile local agents and impressive foreign envoys. Small wonder that they vied with lay lords in the luxury of their lifestyle, the size of their army of servants and the grandeur of their remodelled lodgings - it was many centuries since they had shared the common dormitory and refectory. Expectations had risen too, for some senior monks now lived in individual lodgings and controlled their own accounts. The attractions of hospitality, hawking and hunting were seen by envious secular eyes to have triumphed over the call of the cloister.

Decline

The vast majority of houses could not afford such flamboyance, but even in those much of the physical work was done by servants. Enthusiasm tended to wane, spirituality to lessen, educational standards to fall and discipline to grow lax. Cardinal Wolsey supplied the precedent for the closure of smaller monasteries by obtaining a papal bull in 1524 to dissolve twenty one of them to finance his college at Oxford. A further seven were shut down in 1528-29, and the scene for suppression had almost set itself. The drama that followed was short and decisive.

Fall

Henry VIII needed money and monasteries were temptingly wealthy. A visitation to nearly every religious community was made by a team of royal commissioners, hand-picked by Cromwell, Henry's Vicar General, to gather suitable evidence. Their findings were hasty, incomplete and severe. Genuine abuses were uncovered or spurious ones invented. On the pretext of reform, 243 smaller monasteries with net annual incomes of under £200 were closed down in 1536 by Act of Parliament. All their estates and effects passed to the crown. Life pensions were granted to their superiors and either transfer to a larger foundation or release from their vows was offered to the rest. Only 30% of the total monastic establishment was closed down but this was enough to swell existing unrest into revolt. The suppression issue was one of the many, varied grievances drawn up by northern rebels in the revolt known as the Pilgrimage of Grace. The rebellion was brutally crushed. The abbots of five greater monasteries were tried, found guilty and executed for their treasonable support and their abbeys dissolved. Another supporter, the Abbot of Furness, 'voluntarily'

Thomas Cromwell, Henry VIII's Vicar General

NATIONAL PORTRAIT GALLERY

surrendered his abbey, thus providing a convenient precedent whereby almost all the remaining abbeys, priories, nunneries and friaries fell into royal hands. By 1540 the process of piecemeal surrender was over, the Dissolution complete and monasticism a thing of the past.

Some 1800 to 1900 monks, out of a total of 9000, received no pensions at all and a few were even temporarily imprisoned. The nuns came off worst - they could not become priests, were not supposed to marry (although many did), were less well educated, had fewer marketable skills and their pensions were much smaller. The abbots fared best, with pensions of up to £100 a year, whereas prioresses of some small nunneries got less than many monks.

The king used some abbey stone to strengthen coastal defences, repair old roads and construct new ones. He spent some money on founding schools and colleges and preserved some books and manuscripts in his library. But the wanton damage and destruction were immense. Henry used his gains to pay off debts and finance his wars. Had the Crown retained the land, its profits would have been far greater, but two thirds were sold off before 1547. The real beneficiaries were the new landowners.

Aftermath

Of over 800 monasteries that were closed down, just under a third exist today as substantial buildings. Fourteen great abbeys survived as cathedrals in Henry's new Church of England, the result of his split from Rome. Some churches, or parts of them, became parish churches. Large sections of others, such as the abbot's lodging or the cloister, were converted into great mansions. Others were used as barns, cider stores, breweries, cloth factories and even, at Westminster, as the royal Record Office. Slightly more than a third have been left as ruins, their valuable stone pilfered over the centuries or have been incorporated as parts of other buildings, such as farmhouses. The remaining third have utterly vanished, to be traceable now only from documentary sources, archaeological evidence or aerial photographs.

ENGLISH HERITAGE

**Detail, laver,
Much Wenlock
Priory, Shropshire**

**Hailes Abbey,
Gloucestershire.
S and N Buck, 1732**

ENGLISH HERITAGE

UNDERSTANDING THE SITE

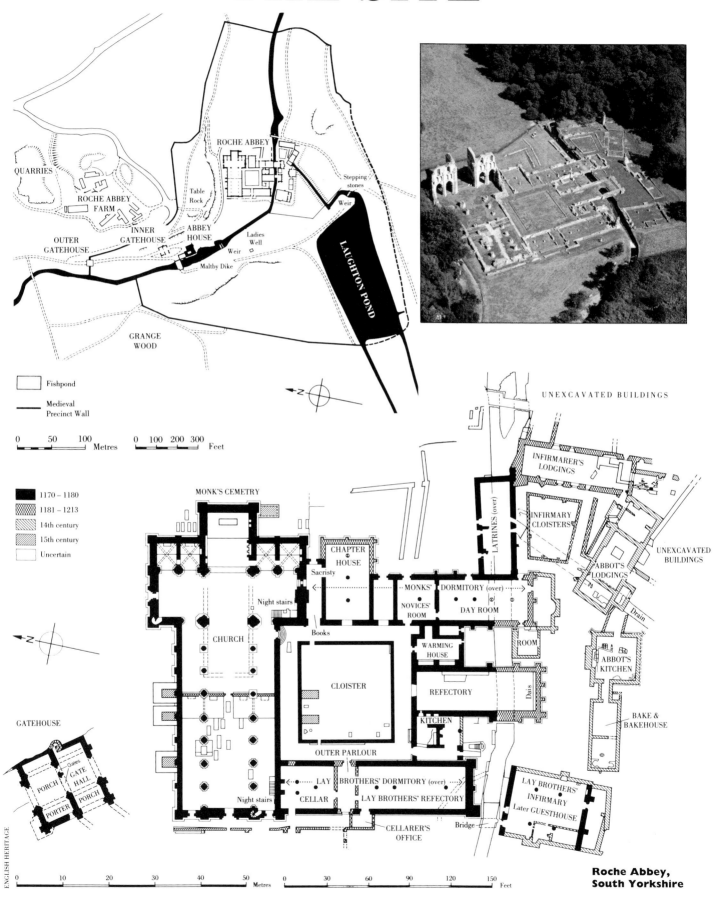

ENGLISH HERITAGE

Fishpond

Medieval Precinct Wall

| 0 | 50 | 100 | Metres |

| 0 | 100 | 200 | 300 | Feet |

1170 – 1180
1181 – 1213
14th century
15th century
Uncertain

QUARRIES

ROCHE ABBEY FARM

ROCHE ABBEY

Table Rock

OUTER GATEHOUSE

INNER GATEHOUSE

ABBEY HOUSE

Maltby Dike

Ladies Well

Weir

Weir

Stepping stones

LAUGHTON POND

GRANGE WOOD

N

MONK'S CEMETERY

CHURCH

Night stairs

Sacristy

CHAPTER HOUSE

Books

MONKS' DORMITORY (over)

NOVICES' ROOM

DAY ROOM

WARMING HOUSE

ROOM

CLOISTER

REFECTORY

Dais

KITCHEN

OUTER PARLOUR

LAY BROTHERS' DORMITORY (over)

Night stairs

CELLAR

LAY BROTHERS' REFECTORY

CELLARER'S OFFICE

Bridge

LATRINES (over)

UNEXCAVATED BUILDINGS

INFIRMARER'S LODGINGS

INFIRMARY CLOISTERS

ABBOT'S LODGINGS

Drain

UNEXCAVATED BUILDINGS

ABBOT'S KITCHEN

BAKE & BAKEHOUSE

LAY BROTHERS' INFIRMARY
Later GUESTHOUSE

GATEHOUSE

PORCH

Gates

GATE HALL

PORCH

PORTER

N

| 0 | 10 | 20 | 30 | 40 | 50 | Metres |

| 0 | 30 | 60 | 90 | 120 | 150 | Feet |

Roche Abbey, South Yorkshire

On arrival at any site you may find mostly footings, broken arches and only a few standing structures, full of blocked doorways and altered windows, but interpreting these is quite straightforward once you realise that almost all abbeys are variations on the same theme. If north is not shown on your plan, remember that the church was usually built on an east-west axis and the line of the east wall was continuous while that of the west wall was broken by one or more entrances. Remember also that the degree of decoration around a doorway is a good indicator of the importance of the room beyond.

Try to absorb the basic shape of the plan of Roche Abbey on the previous page before visiting your site. It is probably more comprehensive than the plan of your monastery for Roche Abbey, as a fully-developed Cistercian community, had to include resident lay brothers, unlike the houses of the earlier Orders. As you approach your abbey, try to assess what natural advantages induced the early monks to choose the site. There must have been a nearby source of water and usually a flattish terrain. Then study your site plan to see if there are any indications of how the laity's approach to the secluded central cloister was restricted by deliberate barriers, such as those at Roche where the **Outer gatehouse** controlled initial entry into the abbey precinct, with perhaps a walled lane running from it to a second barrier, the **Inner or Great gatehouse** which barred access to the cloister. Such gatehouses often had a small gate for pedestrians alongside a larger one for carts. As well as a porter's lodge at ground level, there might have been a courtroom on the first floor. From here entry was gained to the **Outer court**, which contained various outbuildings, usually made of timber for which little evidence

Artist's impression by Judith Dobie of the gatehouse and western part of the precinct, Thornholme Priory, Humberside

generally remains. These included a mill, smithy, barns, stables, tanneries, workshops and sheds for cattle and oxen. Besides these were vegetable gardens, orchards, fishponds, dovecots and possibly a chapel for the laity. Beyond it lay the **Inner court**, which contained the almonry, (where alms were distributed to the poor and sick), guest-houses, granaries, bakehouse and brewhouse. Of course, you may find no trace of any of these features and arrive at the church or cloister by a quite different route from the one originally

Gatehouse, Kirkham Priory, North Yorkshire

Processional door, Lilleshall Abbey, Shropshire

intended. Your best plan is to head straight for the cloister which is usually square in shape with an easily-recognisable central grass courtyard (garth). From here you can orientate the plan with the buildings standing around you. Find the processional doorway in the north-east corner leading into the church (the steps are marked on the large Roche plan with curved lines). Go through the doorway, along to the west end of the **Church** and stand outside to look at the west front, often the most impressive feature of the whole abbey, where the great entrance doors once stood. Sometimes, a narrow porch

that in the Middle Ages there were no pews to restrict the open space, examining the remains of walls and piers and envisaging the huge height and span of the vaulting they once supported. In a Cistercian abbey, look for traces of where the rood screen stood to shut off the lay brothers' western end of the nave from the choir monks' eastern end. Then move to the crossing where the central tower rose up and the transepts, extending north and south, marked the shape of the cross. Look for grave slabs and the remains of chapels, side altars or choir stalls. See if there is any evidence of the high altar or a piscina (stone sink) where the altar

vessels were washed. Is there anything to indicate where the night stairs, used by monks for the night services, gave direct access from the dormitory? Return to the **Cloister** and look for the creasing (band of stone) where the roofs of the four alleys met the surrounding walls. This is where the monks read or copied manuscripts in their carrels (study cubicles) or took exercise in the paved aisles around the cloister garth. Here they had their beards

West Front, Byland Abbey, North Yorkshire

Piscina, Cleeve Abbey, Somerset

Carrels or recesses for monks to work in, Gloucester Cathedral

(Galilee) provided cover here for the ceremonial processions. Walk eastwards up the nave, remembering

Nave, looking east, Rievaulx Abbey, North Yorkshire, with artist's impression by Peter Dunn, on left

trimmed and heads shaved for the tonsure, the emblem of Christ's crown of thorns. Continue clockwise round the cloister to the

East range where the rooms were arranged in functional order. In a Cistercian house like Roche the **Sacristy (vestry)** where the vestments and altar plate were stored, was directly accessible from the south transept. To the west of this was the **Library**, or perhaps just a stone cupboard in the wall or aumbrey (right), where the books were kept close to the sunny north alley, the warmest place to sit. Continue to the

Chapter house, which was the operations room of the abbey, for the daily reading of a chapter of the Rule, the conduct of business and the

Chapter House, Cleeve Abbey, Somerset with artist's impression by Terry Ball, below

administration of punishments. Its importance was shown by a fine carved entrance, often with three openings on to the cloister, symbolic of the Trinity. Look for traces of wall benching where the brethren sat. Move on to the

Inner parlour, where strictly necessary conversation was permitted. Its narrowness reveals a possible second function as a slype (passage), to give access to the even more secluded area east of the cloister. Continue to the

Novices' room, where the novice-master gave tuition and the **Day room,** which the monks used as a common room and covered workroom. Stretching over all the rooms on the east range was the **Dormitory (dorter)** where the monks slept communally in one long

Dorter, or monks' dormitory, Cleeve Abbey, Somerset

room. As their number grew it was sometimes extended beyond the cloister. Your plan may indicate this. Next, look for the **Latrine block (reredorter)** which was directly accessible at ground level from the day room and on the first floor from the dormitory. It might

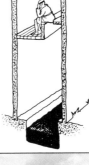

Reredorter, or lavatory, Castle Acre Priory, Norfolk

have been built either over an existing stream or a deliberately-constructed channel. Look for evidence of the drainage channel on your site and work out the direction of flow and destination.

The south range contained the **Warming house** which, until the Rule was relaxed, was the only place where the monks could thaw out by the fire which was kept in all winter. You may find the remains of the huge fireplace(s). Situated near the

Fireplace in warming house, Byland Abbey, North Yorkshire

entrance to the refectory was the **Laver (washing trough)** for the monks to wash their hands before and after meals. Can you work out the routes of the water supply and drainage to and from here? Move on to the

Laver, or washing place, Gloucester Cathedral

Refectory (frater) which was the monks' communal dining hall. In earlier houses it ran lengthwise along the south cloister aisle. In Cistercian

Refectory, Rievaulx Abbey, North Yorkshire with artist's **impression by Alan Sorrell, below**

abbeys it was turned at right angles to provide direct access from the cloister to the warming house and kitchen which were squeezed in alongside. The day stairs were also moved from their usual position immediately south of the chapter house to the east end of the south range, so you may well find signs of re-building here. Inside the refectory, try to locate the position of the wall pulpit - even if no stairs remain, there may be a thickening of a wall. Food was prepared in the kitchen which was located here in Cistercian planning rather than in the west range as in Benedictine convents. In both cases it was up-stream of the reredorter. Look for traces of the fireplaces, drains, cupboards or serving hatch. When the Rule was relaxed a separate meat kitchen was often added, together with its own heated refectory (misericorde). You may find evidence of its later date in the way that it butted up against an existing wall rather than integrated with it.

Sometimes another slype, giving access south of the cloister, was fitted in here. Continue to the **West range** which contained rooms conveniently accessible to the

gatehouse. In the Benedictine Order it was called the Cellarer's range and housed the **kitchen,** as mentioned above, and **cellarium (storeroom)** to which vast quantities of goods could be brought for storage at ground level. It is often recognisable by its lack of windows. Above it was the **Abbot's lodging** where the head of the community had lavish rooms for administrative duties and the entertainment of important guests, who would sleep there or in an adjacent **guest-house.** Later a kitchen, pantry, buttery, bakehouse and brewhouse were added.

Most Orders had some lay brothers but not on the same scale as the Cistercians, which necessitated replanning the west range to fit them in. Some of their lay brothers boarded out at the distant granges (outlying farms). The rest lived in the abbey's west range. Their accommodation comprised the **Lay brothers' refectory,** and sometimes a **day room,** which took up most of the ground floor. Its size gives a clue to the number of lay brothers and the extent of the abbey's estates. Next to this was the **Outer parlour,** where visitors were received. Nearby was the **Cellar,** which provided storage space and the **Cellarer's office,** where accounts were kept.

Above, in the west range, was the Lay brothers' dormitory, which occupied the whole first floor. Its night stairs led directly into the western part of the church to which the lay brothers were restricted. Close at hand was the **Lay brothers' infirmary** - for the sick and old - and beyond that the **Lay brothers' reredorter.** Look for its drainage channel.

The need for the lay brothers' dormitory meant that the Abbot's lodging had to be re-located outside the crowded cloister in a suitably spacious and private spot, often beyond the east range near the **Infirmary,** which was a separate, self-contained complex for the aged and infirm choir monks. It contained the Infirmarer's lodging, a chapel, cloister, dormitory, day room, dining hall and special meat kitchen for those who needed meat to recuperate.

Now that you have the measure of the abbey, take stock. Will your party need a quick explanatory tour or can they be launched straight into action? What possibilities does it offer for group work? If you decide to use groups, how will you ensure that children do not end up knowing everything about something and nothing about everything else? Go round again and take photographs. If it is an English Heritage property, ask if there is an Information Sheet about it or an Education Centre on site.

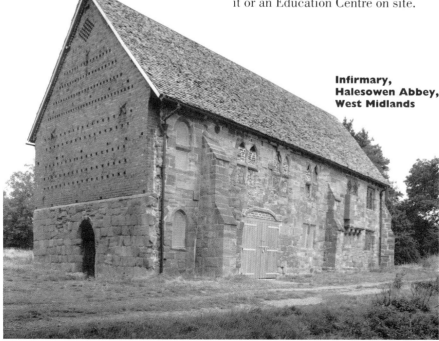

Infirmary, Halesowen Abbey, West Midlands

DAILY LIFE AT THE ABBEY

Daily life in the abbey was structured round eight principal church services. The day was a long one and varied according to season, starting at 1am or 2am and finishing at 6.30pm in winter and later in summer. Timetables differed from Order to Order and abbey to abbey, and even from individual to individual, as some might be excused church services in order to get on with essential duties.

Meals were eaten in silence, listening to a colleague reading from a chosen text. In early Cistercian houses dinner would be a pound of bread and vegetables but other Orders, and later some Cistercians too, included fish, pastry and milk, and on special days wine, poultry, pork and even beef. Supper was a light meal of bread, fruit and ale. An elaborate sign language was used to cope with the enforced silence.

DAILY TIMETABLE IN THE ABBEY

1am   Vigils, Matins and Lauds in church. Return to bed using night stairs.

6am   Prime in church followed by High Mass.

7am   Reading in cloister followed by change from warm night shoes to day shoes in dorter, using day stairs, and wash in cloister.

8am   Tierce in church followed by Mass attended by villagers or guests.

9am   Chapter meeting in chapter house attended by members of abbey only, excluding novices.

10am   Work.

Noon   Sext in church.

1pm   Dinner in refectory.

2pm   Nones in church.

3pm   Study or work.

5pm   Vespers in church and day shoes changed for night shoes in dorter.

5.30pm   Light supper in refectory

6pm   Compline in church.

6.30pm   Bed in dorter

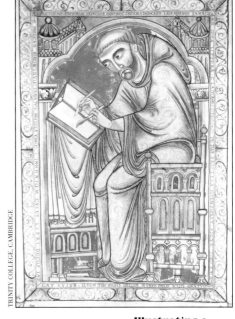

TRINITY COLLEGE, CAMBRIDGE

Illustrating a manuscript

To ensure the smooth running of the abbey a division of labour was necessary. Individuals, known as obedientiaries, were given areas of responsibility; these, and the duties of the ordinary monk or nun, are summarised in the next two pages as 'Who's Who' role cards to photocopy and cut out for use in school or on a site.

BIBLIOTHEQUE MUNICIPALE, DIJON

Manual work, chopping wood.

Abbot or Abbess

Qualities: Virtuous, strict and a good leader.

Duties: Rules the abbey, sets a good example, and is responsible for all spiritual matters, orderly routine and discipline. Takes all services, runs the daily chapter meeting and decides punishments. Carries out a daily inspection of the abbey. Often away on important local and national affairs. When present, entertains noble guests.

Comment: Powerful and sometimes lives like a rich landowner.

Cellarer

Qualities: Prudent, thrifty and good at accounts.

Duties: Senior bursar/steward. Head of abbey's right-hand person, runs all the abbey's business, including its estates and churches. In charge of supplies - food, drink, fuel and materials for repairs. Oversees produce from farms and granges and the payment of bills. Ensures that supplies are correctly stored.

Comment: Very powerful, and often away at the estates. Excused some services because of duties. Has own office and is in charge of the abbey's keys.

Kitchener

Qualities: Good organiser and trustworthy with accounts. Must not be a glutton.

Duties: Catering manager, runs the kitchen and orders all food, beer and wine from the cellarer. Ensures plentiful supplies of fish every Friday. Supervises the head-cook and other servants who do the actual cooking. Keeps daily accounts.

Comment: Sometimes serves vast banquets of splendid quality. Excused some services because of catering duties.

Prior or Prioress

Qualities: Good organiser, efficient and cautious.

Duties: Deputy head, runs the abbey in the abbot's or abbess' absence (in priories is the actual head). In charge of night inspection, rousing the community for services and locking up. Helped by the circator who goes round secretly eavesdropping and reporting those who talk without permission.

Comment: When deputising, is allowed extra food. Chosen with the agreement of the senior monks or nuns.

Fraterer (Refectorian)

Qualities: Punctual, careful and hygienic.

Duties: Steward in charge of the refectory and laver, responsible for their cleanliness. Looks after table linen and candles. In the frater, organises the setting of tables, strewing of clean rushes on floor and washing up. Keeps the kitchen staff quiet during the community's silent meals.

Comment: Excused service after High Mass to supervise the drawing of beer.

Infirmarer

Qualities: Kind, gentle and sympathetic.

Duties: Runs the hospital for temporarily sick monks or nuns, the old and those being bled, who remain three days. Provides suitable diet, including meat if necessary. Skilled in medicine and simple operations. Has herbal remedies always handy. Visits and consoles the sick with prayer and singing while a servant does the actual nursing.

Comment: Is allowed to keep a fire and lamp burning all night.

Almoner

Qualities: Considerate, tactful and patient.
Duties: Gives money and help to the lame, blind, decrepit and bed-ridden at home or admits them to the abbey. Gives out the dole - scraps of food and cast-off clothing. Cares for the comfort of people's souls as well as their bodies.
Comment: Can, without special permission, make visits and has a cash allowance to distribute.

Precentor

Qualities: Good singing voice, dignified and an example to all.
Duties: In charge of church services and music. Leads the singing, selects readers, organises processions and the provision of vestments. Also often acts as tutor/librarian, in charge of all books and manuscripts, book loans, repairs and writing materials.
Comment: As keeper of the abbey records, writes some documents and hires scribes to write others.

Novice-Master/Mistress

Qualities: Patience, firmness, loving care and understanding.
Duties: Responsible for educating and training the young people who want to join the abbey. Stays with them day and night at first and has charge of them for a year. Teaches them to read and write, especially in Latin, and to learn the sign language used when talking is forbidden.
Comment: Shapes the character of the novices and teaches them how to honour God in everything they do.

Guest-Master/Mistress

Qualities: Welcoming, cheerful and thorough.
Duties: Sees that the guest-house has clean, comfortable beds and good meals. Must avoid extravagance and ensure that visitors do not disturb the community. Gets up early to check that guests do not leave anything behind or go off with any of the abbey's linen. Is in charge of transport and oversees the stables and smithy.
Comment: Has to give a good impression of the abbey to the outside world.

Sacristan

Qualities: Accurate, cautious and painstaking.
Duties: Church steward/ security officer in charge of the church contents - relics, altar plate and cloths, vestments, tapers, candles and banners. Also organises repairs and maintenance. Buys wax, tallow and oil for lighting. Responsible for ringing bell to summon the community to services.
Comment: Sleeps in the sacristy to guard precious relics. Is allowed to go to market and fairs to shop, but only with permission.

Monk or Nun

Qualities: Devout, hardworking, obedient.
Duties: Has promised to be obedient at all times, to be poor, and to stay single. Spends the day at worship in church, in studying or copying manuscripts and in skilled work like carving or metalwork, or in manual tasks like gardening.
Comment: Has no personal freedom, but no worries about housing or food, either.

PREPARATION FOR THE VISIT

The first stage is to decide on your objectives, matching them to your overall curriculum requirements. Determine your aims, expected educational outcomes and how you will assess the results. What does the site offer to other areas of the curriculum? Are you using it for its information content, the opportunities it offers to develop skills, as an exemplar of concepts or as a mix of all these? Will the visit be an initial stimulus, a mid-topic motivator or a final high point? How does it fit your personal teaching style? Is it to be an informative backcloth for some specific instruction on your part or more an active learning process by pupils? Check your responses, for now is the time to research documentary evidence, prepare site plans for children and get organised.

Most children have only a vague understanding of an abbey's lifestyle and significance. How much you explain beforehand depends on your intended tactics. If they are to discover things for themselves, only you can judge what would reveal too much. Generally, pupils need enough historical knowledge to appreciate the story of the abbey and to focus on the appropriate period. Specifically, they must know about the Dissolution to understand why many of the buildings are ruined.

It is useful if they can recognise the basic shapes of the main architectural styles.

Prior study of a building site reveals how foundations give clues about the layout of buildings. The class can be introduced to ground plans and be accustomed to the lack of complete buildings on site using a small lift-off clay model of the abbey, or a larger shoe-box model, placed over a ground plan.

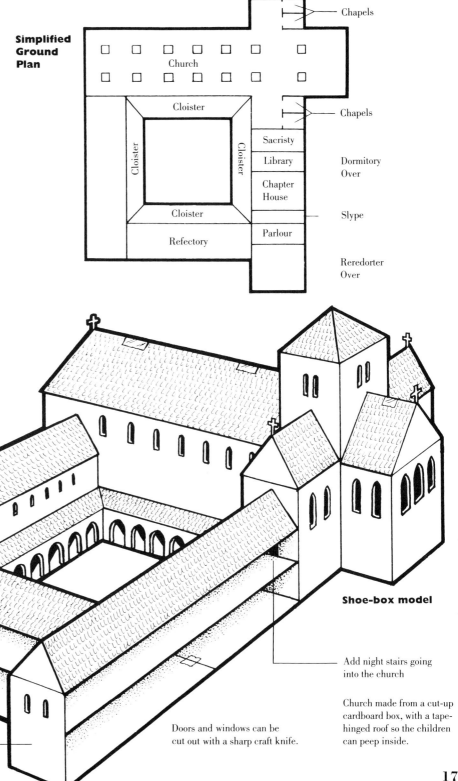

Simplified Ground Plan

Church

Chapels

Cloister

Cloister

Cloister

Cloister

Sacristy

Library

Chapter House

Parlour

Refectory

Chapels

Dormitory Over

Slype

Reredorter Over

Shoe-box model

Card taped in to make an 'upstairs'.

Shoe boxes open at the back can be cut and taped together to get the desired length.

Doors and windows can be cut out with a sharp craft knife.

Add night stairs going into the church

Church made from a cut-up cardboard box, with a tape-hinged roof so the children can peep inside.

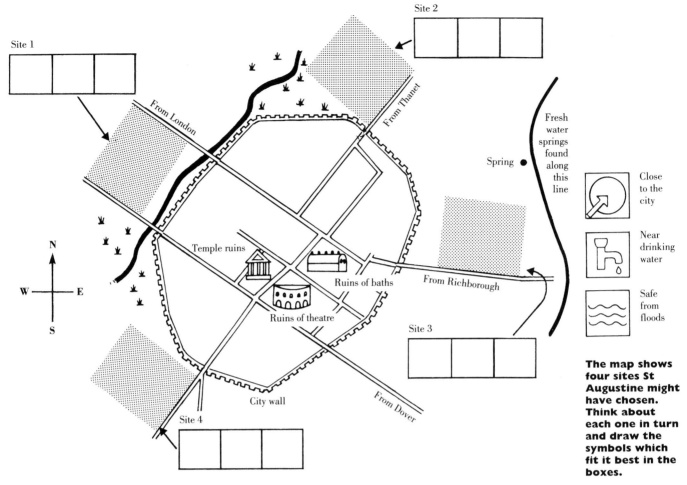

Site 1

Site 2

From London

From Thanet

N
W — E
S

Temple ruins

Ruins of baths

Ruins of theatre

From Richborough

Spring •

Fresh water springs found along this line

Close to the city

Near drinking water

Safe from floods

City wall

From Dover

Site 3

Site 4

The map shows four sites St Augustine might have chosen. Think about each one in turn and draw the symbols which fit it best in the boxes.

Pupils need to be familiar with the concept of location to understand why an abbey is situated where it is. Take St Augustine, having to choose his site at Canterbury. Let the pupils select the best place.

Gradient and flow are useful concepts to examine in advance to help students understand the abbey's water supply and drainage systems which were very sophisticated for their day. The fresh water was drawn off upstream and channelled underground through lead pipes to a large storage tank which fed the kitchens, infirmary and laver. Alternatively, the river was divided to provide one stream of clean water and

another as a foul drain for the huge reredorters. These latrine blocks had to be large because the strict timetabling meant that the monks all tended to arrive at the same time! The gradient had to be correct for the system to function properly.

Pupils should appreciate that abbeys were industrial centres as well as 'powerhouses of prayer', producing tiles, pottery, glass, parchment, beer, honey, leather goods and metalwork. Point out that they once led the field in sanitation, medicine, bee-keeping, fish-farming, horse-breeding, agriculture, wool production and estate management.

ENGLISH HERITAGE

Drain, Cleeve Abbey, Somerset

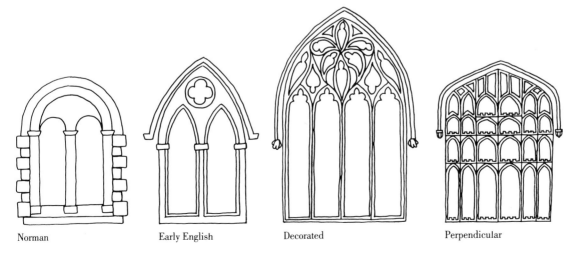

Norman

Early English

Decorated

Perpendicular

Architectural styles

USING THE SITE

SORTING IT OUT

Aims To examine the layout of an abbey and reveal the functional relationship of its parts.
Concepts Design, function, scale, shape, change, similarity, difference.
Skills Reading and drawing of plans, recognition of compass points, recording by notes, sketches and photographs, measurement, deduction, hypothesis.

Preparation

Before going on site a grasp of the concept of function is necessary. Can the class suggest what buildings a community of monks or nuns would need for themselves and for caring for the sick, poor and travellers? To illustrate the connection between function and design draw up a ground plan of the school and make a list of the activities that take place there, adding to it any extra ones that took place in an abbey. How does function determine room size and interior decoration in school? This is a good opportunity to introduce the correct names for parts of the abbey.

On Site

Suit your tactics to the pupils' abilities and the site's complexities. The following suggestions are intended to make pupils work out for themselves the nature and function of the buildings.

Which is which?

Distribute blank outline plans, with North indicated, and allocate small groups a room each, or give them a photograph with which to identify their part of the site. They can discover its function by studying the outline shapes and remaining features, such as fireplaces, ovens and drains, and remembering points such as access and water supply and relative size. Having decided, they make detailed observational drawings of the buildings and number them on their plans. Let them present their conclusions to the rest of the class, but do not divulge the names of the rooms until they have grasped the functions. Older pupils, able to cope with long measuring tapes, triangulation and working to scale, could make their own plans, either of a room or a building, and compare them afterwards with the official plan.

Who goes where?

Give out role cards. The pupils identify the appropriate building for the character or, if it is missing, decide where it would have been and, if possible, mark it out. They then either sketch the actual remains or describe what facilities would have existed.

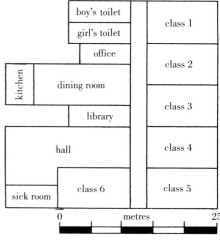

How does the plan of an abbey compare with that of a school?

Activity	Code	School	St Augustine's
work		classroom	cloister
eating		dining room	frater
cooking		kitchen	kitchen
assembly		hall	chapter house
church services			abbey church/chapels
going to the toilet		toilets	reredorter
illness		sick room	infirmary
reading		library	library
sleeping			dorter
walking		corridor	passage
administration		office	abbot's lodgings

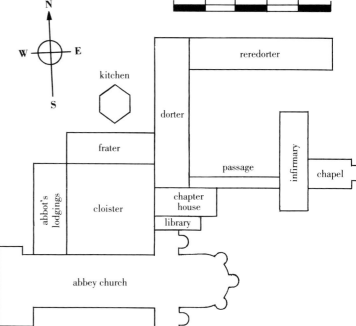

Complete the code boxes using a different colour code for each activity

Colour the plans of school and the abbey using the code you have chosen

Spot the difference

Distribute 'then and now' sheets containing photocopies of old prints and photographs to illustrate how the buildings formerly looked. Pupils locate the sites, sketch the existing structures, identify the building and note the changes.

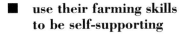

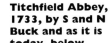

Titchfield Abbey, 1733, by S and N Buck and as it is today, below

Complete the puzzle

Distribute large jig-saw pieces of the site plan which the children have already mounted on thick card and cut out in class. Each group receives a piece containing one or more buildings and has to locate the area and make a full labelled sketch of it before claiming the next piece.

Follow up with searching questions. What is the lie of the land? How does this relate to the routes of fresh water supply and the waste drainage? Where were these needed? Where were the fishponds, vegetable gardens and abbey mill, if there was one? Which were the the most impressive

buildings and why? Assess the size of the windows, doors and interiors and the amount of decorative detail. Use a matrix, giving possible scores out of ten.

At some point, check the pupils' grasp of the layout of the site by making a pre-arranged signal for them

to return to the cloister at a time when they are dispersed all over the abbey. They must make their way back by the most appropriate routes, using only actual doorways which either still exist or are marked out on their plans, but not take any short cuts over footings or low walls.

Follow up

Compare the abbey site with the school plan and consider how they reflect the priorities and organisation of both societies. Ask how far their interpretation of the site is distorted by its incompleteness. Introduce any relevant primary or secondary sources.

Most pupils will have seen nuns, if not monks, and may wonder why they are here at all if every abbey was closed down. Explain that centuries later monks and nuns returned from abroad to build new abbeys.

Discuss how a modern monastery might differ from the site they visited: the churches may be similar, but blocks of study-bedrooms often replace the earlier cloisters and dormitories. Encourage debate on how present day monastic communities can survive financially and become a part of their surrounding communities. The pupils ought to be able to suggest some of these alternatives:

- **use their farming skills to be self-supporting**

- **use their craft skills for profit** *pottery, stained glass, metalwork*
  Prinknash Abbey(Glos)
  wine
  Buckfast Abbey (Devon)
  perfume
  Caldey Abbey (S.Wales)
  honey
  Lindisfarne Priory (Northumberland)
  embroidery
  Turvey Priory (Beds)

- **use their educational skills** *run a school*
  Ampleforth (Yorks)

- **run a students' hostel**
  Greyfrairs (Oxford)

- **run a conference centre**
  Aylesford Friary (Kent)

- **use their social skills** *run a retreat*
  Mount St Bernard Abbey (Leics)
  support a hospice
  Willen Priory (Milton Keynes)

- **use their spiritual training in general social work**

The class might end their discussion by considering the future of the welfare state and free education and how the poor, aged and infirm should be cared for in our society.

PEOPLING THE SITE

Aims To heighten understanding and awareness of monastic life.
Concepts Similarity, difference, change, bias, imagination.
Skills Observation, empathetic understanding, imaginative reconstruction.

Finding the human dimension can be achieved through role play or tightly structured investigations.

Preparation for role play

Researching and making costume is useful but not essential. What is vital is a good understanding of the monastic timetable: making an interactive or clockface timetable will help. Or pupils could make an accurate drawing or clay model of a monk or nun, and, working through the twenty-four hour timetable, move it to the appropriate place on a large, labelled ground plan of the site. This highlights the time spent in prayer and emphasises the need for servants, hired craftsman and lay brethren. Photocopy the Who's Who role cards (younger pupils can illustrate them on the back with appropriate symbols of office). Try role play in school first, perhaps eating or working in silence, using sign language. If pupils are to re-enact tasks or skills, make sure that they research the processes and the appropriateness of the artefacts thoroughly. If they are to be confronted with an incident on site, they must understand, in advance, the issues involved to deal with it.

On site

Try a chapter house meeting with a reading of the Rule, an allocation of tasks and an investigation into any wrong-doing. Allocate the obedientiaries' roles to self-reliant pupils who might help less confident ones. Incidents can include a visitation by the bishop to inspect the community, or the arrival of pilgrims bringing news of the outside world and possibly, inadvertently, the Black Death. The issue of Henry VIII's destruction of the monasteries can be introduced by the appearance of fault-finding Commissioners, which can be followed up by the arrival of the new owner or locals carrying away building materials. Consider how to

return to reality: pupils need to know when they officially return to the present, but this needs handling with sensitivity.

Follow up

Encourage research, imaginative writing, artwork and practical work into facets of medieval life such as diet and cooking, medicine or craft processes like tile-making. Have primary and secondary evidence available to answer questions on monastic finance.

Make an abbey timetable

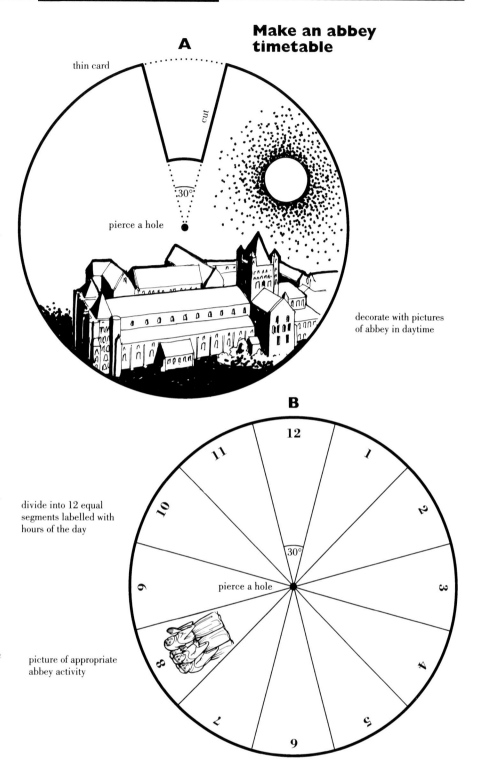

A

thin card

cut

30°

pierce a hole

decorate with pictures of abbey in daytime

B

12
11 · 1
10 · 2
30°
9 · pierce a hole · 3
8 · 4
7 · 5
9

divide into 12 equal segments labelled with hours of the day

picture of appropriate abbey activity

Attach 'A' over 'B' with split pin paper fastener at centre.

Follow similar procedure for night-time timetable. Alternatively obedientiaries timetables can be made, with 'A' decorated with typical tasks and 'B' with sketches made on site of the associated locations.

Preparation for imaginative writing

When pupils are familiar with the abbey's daily timetable, they should be encouraged to discuss what such a rigid structuring of the day entails, perhaps by comparing it with their own lifestyles.

Discuss why someone should want to give up normal life to enter a monastery. What does it mean to live by a Rule? Lead this into talking about the advantages and disadvantages of communal life. Ask pupils to draw up a rough list of the different work that needs to be done, like looking after the money or food, and compare it to the Who's Who list. Photocopy and cut up the Who's Who page into individual descriptions.

On Site

Divide the class into pairs or small groups and give each a Who's Who card, a labelled plan and a copy of the daily timetable. Decide on a framework for the strategy. It may be that pupils are collecting notes to write a newspaper interview with a monk at the time of the Dissolution, a diary entry, a video storyboard, a taped commentary for use on site or some other piece of imaginative writing. Tell them to visit those buildings used by their Who's Who character and go back to the place most associated with the character to write down information about the area, such as name, size, nearby rooms, large doors, small windows, tiled floors, grey walls, etc. When they have done that, tell them to make their way to the church, using only the actual doorways or paths around buildings. In the church let them suggest how it might have looked and sounded and how they might have felt in it. They may feel happier doing this if you give them a choice of words to select from and adding one of their own.

Ask them to return to their original room and, after studying their Who's Who card, to decide if their character would have worked alone, like the cellarer; with others, like the precentor; or alone but meeting others, like the almoner. What do they personally consider would have been good or bad about the job – meeting people from the outside, working alone, or being near the kitchen fire in winter? What would they have heard or seen nearby? They could question different groups working near them about what other characters did.

Remind them that the Dissolution swept this lifestyle away at a stroke. Ask them to note down how they think their characters would have survived outside the abbey; had they any marketable skills and what were they? How would they personally feel in a similar situation - angry, apprehensive, resigned or resentful?

They may wish to describe their monk or nun. Tell them to keep this to a minimum and to make any physical descriptions reflect the working conditions, like 'hands red from cold' or 'face flushed from the heat of fire'.

Follow up

In school the class could discuss what extra information would make their piece of work more interesting, for instance, the character's name, clothes, and physical features, more details about work, what was eaten for breakfast, or what pension was received on leaving the abbey. Can they distinguish between what can be researched in primary or secondary sources and what must be invention? This is a good opportunity to introduce the differences between the two types of source. The class could speculate on what the monks and nuns might have done after the Dissolution. With prompting they might produce a list like this:

- continue as before, but in private communities - a few did, mostly nuns

- live on their pensions - about £5 a year for a monk

- become priests in parish churches or chantries – private chapels endowed by families for the saying of prayers for the dead

- return home and look for other work

- become chaplains or tutors in noblemen's houses

- use their reading, writing and accounting skills as clerks

- go abroad, where monasteries had not been closed down

Research may throw up different verdicts on the monks' fate - legitimately so, as the treatment was not at all uniform. Pupils can be introduced to the idea of bias by considering how accounts of the Dissolution would differ if recorded by a poor nun, a well-pensioned abbot, or the new owner of a monastic site.

At Key Stage 2

large	dark	small	bright	
hot	cold	warm	chilly	
chanting	shuffling	coughing	creaking	
calm	bored	sleepy	joyful	

At Key Stage 3

intimidating	uplifting	majestic	gloomy	
suffocating	airy	draughty	oppressive	
resonant	restful	shrill	sweet	
elated	still	content	invigorated	

RECOGNISING CHANGE

Aims To examine the nature of physical evidence and how to hypothesise from it.
Concepts Change, cause and effect, sequence, stratigraphy, evidence.
Skills Observation, orientation, recording with notes, sketching and photography, analysis, interpretation.

Preparation

At the abbey, pupils will find evidence of change; they need to grasp the causes and consequences. Prepare them by logging the slow decay in some derelict structure or considering what their classroom would look like after a hundred years' neglect. To reveal the rapid effects of structural changes, ask them to design a home extension. What differences would this make to the original building? Would there be blocked doorways or windows? What evidence would remain visible and what would be covered over? Might the new windows and doors show any changes of style?

Prior's lodging, Monk Bretton, South Yorkshire

ENGLISH HERITAGE

On Site

You need measuring tapes, cameras, clinometers, metre rules or ranging poles and a labelled plan. The aim is for pupils to find evidence of change, accurately survey and record it, then analyse and interpret it - the same process that archaeologists and detectives use. Allocate groups to areas and ensure that they mark their location on the overall plan.

Find, survey, record Pupils should look for clues which show that earlier features have now disappeared.

Incomplete walls or stairs, or fireplaces and doors high up on walls all indicate the position of former floors. Corbels projecting from the walls once supported roof beams and socket holes reveal where these slotted into the stones. Encourage pupils to look closely at holes and rebates (grooves cut to receive an edge) to work out what they originally held, perhaps window bars or door fittings. Evidence of changes made deliberately to the building, like blocked doorways or inserted windows, reveal past modernisation. Extensions are indicated by obvious breaks in the masonry (where walls butt up against each other rather than follow the normal pattern of integrated bonding) by sudden,

otherwise inexplicable, alterations in floor levels.

Parts of the site may be lived in or have evidence of post-Dissolution change. These may be inaccessible for detailed work, but noting changes in their facades is important for an overall view of change at the abbey.

All evidence should be recorded by numbered drawings or photographs, then measured, and its position marked on the ground plan.

Analyse and interpret What does the evidence suggest to pupils about the properties of the material from which a missing feature might have been made? For example, was it easily cut, heavy, light? Is there any evidence of remaining material to help them? What do they think happened to the material – decay, or re-use and why? What do they think the material was?

What do the location and surrounding features indicate – marks left by a former roof or arch might mean that the wall has been changed from an interior to an exterior one. Can they date their feature by its relationship to other changes? For example, a window built into a blocked arch must be later than the arch. Can they date it by referring to a style guide?

They can also test for relative strength by shattering techniques – behind a screen, within a box or by dropping weights down a tube. Insist on the use of protective goggles. Let them see how samples react to repeated immersion, freezing and thawing. Bury different materials and later check their comparative rate of decomposition.

They might discuss whether the abbey is in danger of further deterioration, perhaps from acid rain, and ask what should be done about it. This can lead into a debate about a whole series of conservation issues and the value and cost of conserving historic monuments.

Church made into private dwellings, Bury St Edmunds Abbey, Suffolk

Follow up

Pupils could devise and carry out experiments on properties of materials. Ask them to bring in samples of different types of stone for close examination at school. They can test for solubility by immersion in vinegar or a weak solution of acid.

Walls butting up, Lilleshall Abbey, Shropshire

Denny Abbey, Cambridgeshire

SEEING IT AS IT WAS

Aims To alert pupils to a variety of sources in looking for evidence. **Concepts** Size, shape, volume, area, angles, tessellation, symmetry, scale, proportion, forces, change, function. **Skills** Observation, calculation, estimation, surveying, working to scale, recording, deduction, analysis, hypothesis.

Preparation

This activity calls for accuracy in measuring and ability to work to scale. A knowledge of familiar mathematical shapes is needed to help in analysing an elevation - the triangle for the apex, the rectangle or square for the wall, the circle for the rose window and the semi-circle and arcs for the arches in doorways and windows. Recognition of symmetry is helpful as it provides clues to the abbey's appearance : transepts stand opposite each other and windows are designed about their lines of symmetry - a useful point to remember when trying to envisage the whole of some shattered tracery. Pupils will also need to know about tesselation to work out how medieval tile pavements were designed. Squared paper helps them to set out the more complicated relationships. They can also use the tiles to calculate area.

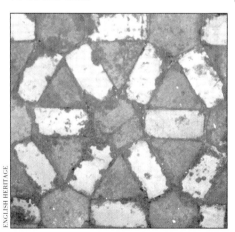

ENGLISH HERITAGE

Rievaulx Abbey, North Yorkshire

If there is building work going on near school ask pupils to attempt their own sketches of an elevation by drawing a projection upwards from the base of a part-built wall.

You may wish their impressions of the complete abbey to be represented in detailed drawings or in a model, but scale needs to be decided on first. Pupils may need practice in drawing in three-dimensions and model – makers can gain self-confidence by making simple structures in card.

On site

First, ask pupils to survey the various types of building materials, noting their colour, shape, and texture. They may find that different stone was selected for quoins (corner stones or keystones), or windows or carvings, or that patterns of bonding stones vary. Discuss why.

Next, divide the class into groups to survey different parts of the site.

ENGLISH HERITAGE

The groups should contain:
- **measurers** - who use tapes to find the dimensions of all walls and buttresses. They should also measure salient features, such as arch spans and pillar circumferences
- **artists** - who make careful drawings of the outlines of the structures, including the different buttresses. They should sketch the variously-shaped arches, pillars and windows. Using squared paper will help them to get the proportions right and to plot specific items accurately
- **photographers** - record any features which the artists find difficult to complete in time
- **recorders** - who keep tabulated notes of all the measurements, photographs and sketches, and who act as group leaders

Each group, working as a unit, should consider the structural implications of large windows and heavy roofs. Can they suggest what took the thrust of the roof's weight, how buttresses worked and which is the strongest type of arch? They should reach a joint conclusion on any necessary estimations - such as the original height of missing pillars, fallen walls and the pitch of a lost roof. They should consider what windows, doors and decorative features there may have been and what materials they would have been made of, so that they finally agree what the building once looked like. They should look at other buildings on site for extra clues and then record their conclusions, however inaccurate, by a sketch, diagram or description. Ask them to make a list of things they need to find out, perhaps the size of the buttress gives a clue to the height of the wall.

Follow up

Using their research list, pupils can use reference books to acquire information or conduct their own experiments – on forces exerted downwards on walls or on how buttresses and vaults function and how these relate to the height of walls. There may be other questions – why do arc shapes predominate over straight lintels in doors or why are particular bonding patterns used in walls?

Pictures of similar sites, old prints of their site, artists' impressions of the original buildings and visits to complete buildings, such as churches, will all help pupils to answer questions and visualise their own site.

If the class plans to make a model, provide an enlarged ground plan and ask them to break down their sketches into three-dimensional solids, such as cuboids and triangular prisms. They need to make these up in card to an agreed scale and exact measurements. If they decide on reconstruction drawings, they have a choice of elevations

or more difficult perspective work. In either case individuals can become responsible for certain features within their group, for example, one pupil might be responsible for drawing the pattern of stone work

(for model-makers this can be photocopied and used as cladding), whilst another might be responsible for drawing correctly scaled versions of windows. Working in this way can lift pupils to different levels of perception and enquiry.

Castle Acre Priory, Norfolk

SOLVING PROBLEMS

The principle is to make students responsible for solving an invented but realistic problem, thus strengthening their motivation and heightening their sense of achievement. It is important to determine beforehand what aspect you wish the pupils to examine and only then to create the frame through which they view it. The question should lead pupils to work out a solution through discussion and debate.

You have been asked to design a cafe which is to be built in the grounds. It must:

■ be conveniently placed for visitors but not interfere with a tour of the abbey

■ reflect the style of the abbey, inside and outside, in shape, windows, doors, etc

■ be large enough to accommodate twenty people

Take photographs, make drawings of windows, doors, decorative features and materials which you want to include in your design. Decide where you want your cafe to be built and mark it on the ground plan.

Follow up
Draw your design. Next, design furniture and crockery to match your building. Research monastic food and adapt the recipes for snacks to serve in the cafe.

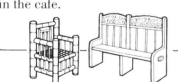

It is felt that the abbey site is not explained clearly enough for five and six year olds. You have been given the job of interpreting the site for this age group.

There are several points to bear in mind:

■ what you think they should know about the site

■ what you think will interest them most

■ what language and reading limitations there will be

■ how long their concentration span is

Write a report with examples of your ideas. These might include pictures on panels, a simple guide book, interactive displays, a guided tour, a tape, etc.

Follow up
Design and make an inexpensive souvenir for this age of visitor to buy in the shop.

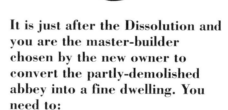

It is just after the Dissolution and you are the master-builder chosen by the new owner to convert the partly-demolished abbey into a fine dwelling. You need to:

■ decide what rooms will be needed in the new dwelling

■ draw up a full survey plan of the site to show present buildings and access routes and water supply

■ decide which area is the most suitable for the new building, explaining which rooms can be easily converted or rebuilt and if new building is necessary

Follow up
Research what the interiors of monastic and secular dwellings looked like to provide sketches to accompany your report.

Write a letter to a friend from:

■ a monk who used to live at the site relating the changes in its appearance and use

■ the new owner commenting on the advantages of his new residence, like easily available stone, established garden, good sanitation.

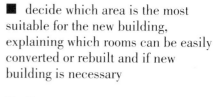

A road is planned which will pass through the abbey site, but its exact route has not been decided. You have been asked to draw up a report to advise the planners. You need to:

■ survey the whole site

■ decide what route will do least damage (to the buildings, or to the atmosphere, or to an understanding of the site) and explain why.

Your report should also include what effect you think the road will have:

■ on the site

■ on the visitors' enjoyment of it

Follow up
An alternative route has been suggested but it will use the land put aside for a recreation field. Write a letter to your local paper supporting one of the routes as:

■ a parent of a child who plays in the street because there is nowhere else

■ a resident living near the abbey

■ someone who feels the abbey is an important part of the area's history.

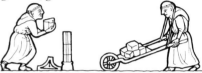

ABBEYS AND THE NATIONAL CURRICULUM

HISTORY

Sitework encourages historical enquiry, from the simplest verbal question to more complex investigations involving detailed surveys, field notes and drawings. It is often most productive to ask pupils to work in groups or pairs, which leads to discussion and resolution.

Even very young children can understand the concepts of change and continuity when they are presented in a concrete form, like the shape and function of windows.

Older pupils can be asked to sequence changes. Features like heating, cooking and sanitary arrangements can be compared to those from other historical periods. Sites allow pupils to understand that change can lead to incomplete evidence and, consequently, to biased interpretations.

All pupils using a site as an historical source can talk about what they see and draw conclusions from it about how the abbey community lived. Older pupils can test the accuracy of their deductions by referring to documentary sources and, by comparing the two types of evidence, may form a judgment on the advantages and limitations of each. For Key Stage 1 pupils a site is a safe environment for finding out how people in the distant past lived.

At Key Stage 2, studying an abbey site will exemplify the effects of Henry VIII's religious policies and links with the missionary work of Christians in the pre-conquest period and with the religious organisations of other cultures at the time of the great explorations. It can also contribute to units on houses and places of worship, writing and printing and local history.

The role of the abbeys is an integral part of medieval studies at Key Stage 3 and the Dissolution contributes to later work on the making of the United Kingdom.

Key Stage 4 pupils studying Model 2 can use a site as a major contribution to work on historical themes, like religion, medicine, care of the poor and work.

ENGLISH

Using the stimulus of the site itself can encourage imaginative descriptive writing in both prose and poetry. Sitework focuses attention on listening and talking. Working in groups involves a high level of verbal interaction, and often results in spoken presentations to others. Interpreting the site to a wide range of visitors - adults, children, academics or foreign tourists leads pupils to appreciate that writing forms vary accordingly to audience, for example, a display panel, a comic strip, or a taped guide. Transcribing taped commentaries will alert pupils to the difference between written and spoken English.

The different environment of the site will stimulate the use of a wider vocabulary, including historical terms. As so much Latin nomenclature is used to identify parts of the abbey, this can be a good starting point for looking at derivation of words and the history of the language.

Pupils at Key Stage 4 can use the abbey as the focus for a report incorporating different stylistic forms, for example, a feasibility study for a new shop, which would require drawing up a questionnaire and interpreting the results, statistical information, rational argument and a summary.

The results of work done on site in other curriculum areas need to be communicated through English; notes need to be re-drafted and surveys written up as reports. This will demand increasingly sophisticated skills in organising, reconstructing, reviewing and hypothesising; the presentation of the project may involve the use of word-processing or desk-top publishing skills.

SCIENCE

The use and properties of building materials and their susceptibility to weathering and pollution can be noted. Back in school, pupils can use the information to design and carry out experiments, for example, in solubility, hardness, strength, rate of decay, etc.

The techniques used to support walls bearing heavy roofs can be noted and experiments carried out in school on the forces involved. Similarly, the predominance of the arc shape in doors and vaulting can be noted and experiments to test its strength devised.

Sites are convenient places for looking at plants as they provide a variety of growing conditions.

An arch being built and tested by the placing of weights on top of it

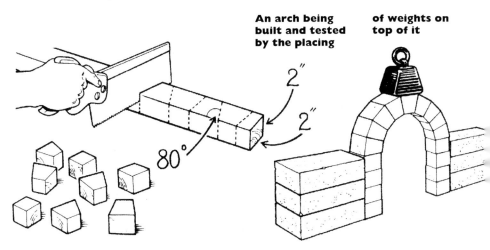

TECHNOLOGY

Abbey sites provide pupils of all ages with the required out-of-school context in which to explore a variety of materials, artefacts and systems and to identify design opportunities. It also provides examples of how technological problems were addressed by people in the past. Pupils might work out the relationships between tall walls, large windows and buttresses and between the spacing of pillars and height in vaulted rooms and ask why arch shapes were commonly used. They could investigate the forces involved and the solutions employed by the medieval builders. This might then be followed up by research into building methods. The pupils could discover how problems like the provision of a fresh water supply, sanitation, heating and lighting were dealt with.

Opportunities for design can arise out of the need to interpret the site to others, including handicapped people, through signs, guidebooks, textured ground plans, interactive displays, etc. Older pupils might use the site as the basis for evaluating the opportunity for better or different facilities, perhaps by collating information from a questionnaire they have devised, and bearing in mind environmental, economic, social, moral and legal considerations. Accurate models of the site and scenery, costumes, or props for a play can be produced. Tile making and design could be researched and replicas made as souvenirs for the site shop, with consideration of costs and marketing strategies.

Follow up activities can include research into medieval medicine and cooking.

Novices' Room, Battle Abbey, Sussex

ENGLISH HERITAGE

Tile making

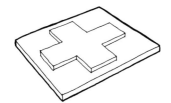

Glue thick card shapes onto card.

Cut a square from a slab of clay.

Press the design into the clay and fill the indentations with slip.

Glaze and fire tile.

If self-hardening clay is used, paint tile brown, and when dry fill indentations with uncoloured clay. Varnish when dry.

MATHEMATICS

Sites provide numerous opportunities for measuring and estimating in length, area, volume, time and weight. Measurements may be used to make drawings, elevations and ground plans to scale. Calculating the volume of a wall can give pupils a realistic idea of the enormous effort involved in transporting material. Making drawings or models calls for work with space and shapes, symmetry and tesselation.

Pupils can utilise mathematical language (diagonal, curved, etc) and knowledge of angles, together with the use of a compass, by describing routes round the abbey in mathematical terms only. Other class members could test their results.

Working out the ratio of window size to wall thickness will provide important data for work on buttresses.

Time was an important feature of monastic life but there is little evidence about clocks on sites. Mathematics can be used and applied in designing alternative means of keeping time, using trial and improvement methods, such as an egg timer, a water clock or a sundial.

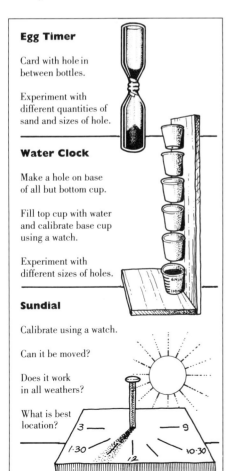

Egg Timer

Card with hole in between bottles.

Experiment with different quantities of sand and sizes of hole.

Water Clock

Make a hole on base of all but bottom cup.

Fill top cup with water and calibrate base cup using a watch.

Experiment with different sizes of holes.

Sundial

Calibrate using a watch.

Can it be moved?

Does it work in all weathers?

What is best location?

GEOGRAPHY

Pupils can relate what they see to ground plans, adding pictures, symbols or colour coding, with keys. A numbered grid placed over the plan gives practice in locating by co-ordinates. Compasses are essential in making up or following accurate directions for routes around the site.

Older pupils might survey the site – its location, terrain and water supply, and then surmise why it was chosen, checking their findings on an ordinance survey map.

The causes and effects of weathering and pollution on buildings could be investigated. Building materials might be examined and their place of origin and route to the site checked on maps.

The role of the abbey in the surrounding settlement can be investigated, perhaps as a tourist attraction which affects the local economy, communications systems and quality of life.

MODERN LANGUAGES

Written work could include a postcard home from a foreign visitor to the abbey, translating or writing an informative leaflet, writing a descriptive sentence or paragraph about a photograph or designing and writing an explanatory display panel for use on site.

Oral work could arise from making a taped commentary for foreign visitors or from providing a voice-over for a video or tape-slide presentation to show in school.

MUSIC

Abbeys are often tranquil sites and therefore good places for composing and performing music.

Sound pictures based on the buildings, the pattern of the monk's day or the history of the site can be composed and performed. Listening to plainsong on site is an evocative experience and can be a starting point for studying the history of music. Plainsong was originally a device to ensure that the monks or nuns sang in time together. Older pupils might analyse the variations that were added on to this simple form, whilst younger ones could compare it to other chants, like football or 'working'

songs. It can also be compared to modern Christian music like hymns and sung masses or to religious music from other cultures, like the Muslim call to prayer.

RELIGIOUS EDUCATION

Abbeys are an essential part of European religious history. The function of the buildings reflect the spiritual and wide practical interpretation of Christianity. They

Representation of a chalice, denoting a priest, inscribed on to grave slab in church of Monk Bretton Priory, South Yorkshire

ENGLISH HERITAGE

offer good starting points for comparison with present day attitudes and with other religions.

ART

Sites are a safe and stimulating place for pupils to draw from first hand experience or take photographs for photo-montage work.

It is easiest to use dry materials, like chalks, charcoal, pencils and crayons but the effect can be varied by using different colours and qualities of paper. Younger pupils could use a hand lens or a viewfinder to focus in on their subject or they can experiment with simple perspectives by drawing a dramatic feature from different angles or distances.

Key Stage 2 and 3 pupils can concentrate on shapes by drawing, in silhouette if they wish, different parts of the site which could be put together at school to form a panorama. They could find examples of repetition, sequence and symmetry in patterns of stonework or carving and discuss the colours they see in terms of tones, warmth, coolness and complementary qualities.

Pupils might be asked to sketch or photograph an image on site which they feel best reflects the atmosphere of the place. They could refine this into a poster using a different medium or printing technique.

CROSS-CURRICULAR ELEMENTS

Effective sitework calls for highly developed skills but these do not always rely heavily on advanced reading or writing ability. Information can be recorded by drawings, photographs, video or tapes which enables pupils of different abilities, including those with special needs or for whom English is a second language, to have an equal opportunity to undertake and satisfactorily complete sitework.

Abbey sites increase economic and industrial understanding if investigated as part of the culture and leisure industries. This encourages investigation of different jobs and career opportunities in maintaining and presenting the site to the public.

For pupils following a course in health education abbey sites are useful in showing how fresh water supplies and sanitation were previously dealt with and how the sick were provided for.

ENGLISH HERITAGE

Repairing and replacing roof timbers at Halesowen Abbey, West Midlands

Views for and against preserving the site and related conservation issues may be debated, opening up the concept of responsibility towards the environment which pupils will later exercise as adults.

Beverly Minster, by Benjamin Roebuck, aged 10.

DOCUMENTARY SOURCES

It is best to begin your research by reading the guidebook history. The local history librarian at your Reference Library and the archivist at your Record Office will know the primary and secondary sources and any available transcriptions. They may also be able to recommend experts who might save you hours of time. The Planning Authority may supply photocopies of large scale maps of the abbey's vicinity. The local Archaeological Unit, if there is one, or the nearest Museum, keeps a record of all nearby excavations and can advise on the whereabouts of any finds. The transactions of antiquarian and archaeological societies and volumes of the Victoria County History look dull but are often full of fascinating detail and convenient translations from original sources. These may include:

■ the rules and observances of the different Orders

■ entries in the bishops' Registers, especially injunctions sent out after visitations

■ monastic account books, with details of fees and wages, records of court cases, etc

■ agreements about land transactions

■ inventories, especially at the time of the Suppression

■ letters, chronicles, biographies and autobiographies written by monks and wills of former monks

If you intend to use documents for a study in evidence, then the period of the Dissolution is your best choice, for its wide range of primary sources and secondary studies. The last two extracts are both primary sources relating directly to monasteries at the Dissolution.

The Benedictine Rule:
(sixth century)

Idleness is the enemy of the soul. For this reason the brethren should be occupied at certain times in manual labour, and at other times in sacred reading. Loose talk, idle words and talk that stimulates laughter, we condemn this with a permanent ban in all places and we do not allow a disciple to open his mouth in this kind of speech. At all times monks ought to strive to keep silence but particularly so during the hours of the night when they come out of Compline there should be no further permission for anyone to talk about anything. No one may take it upon himself to possess anything as his own, anything whatever, books or writing tablets or pen or anything at all, for they are not allowed to retain at their own disposition their own bodies or wills. It is sufficient for a monk to have two tunics and two cowls, to allow for wear at night and for washing. Those who are sent on a journey should get drawers from the wardrobe, which they should wash and give back on their return. All should sleep in one place. The younger brethren should not have their beds together but dispersed among the seniors. For bedding, a mattress, a blanket, a coverlet and a pillow are enough. The beds should be frequently inspected by the Abbot as a precaution against private possessions. For the daily meal there should always be two cooked dishes. And if fruit or tender vegetables are to be had, a third dish may be added. A full pound of bread should be enough for a day. All must refrain entirely from eating the flesh of quadrupeds, except for the sick who are really weak. All who arrive as guests are to be welcomed like Christ.

The Rule of Saint Benedict, translated by D. Parry.

Wayward nuns

...some of the nuns...bring with them to church birds, rabbits, hounds... whereunto they give more heed than to the offices of the church... therefore we strictly forbid you...that ye presume henceforward to bring to Church no birds, hounds, rabbits... as through hunting dogs and other hounds abiding within your monastic precincts, the alms that should be given to the poor are devoured and the church and cloister are foully defiled... through the inordinate noise divine service is frequently troubled - therefore we strictly command... you, Lady Abbess, that you remove the dogs altogether.

Bishop's injunction to the Abbess of Romsey 1387

Nuns returning to the abbey after a night of dissipation

The spoiling of Roche Abbey

It would have made an Heart of Flint to have melted and weeped to have seen the breaking up of the House, and their sorrowfull departing; and the sudden spoil that fell the same day...And every Person had every thing good cheap; except the poor Monks, Fryers, and Nuns that had no Money to bestow of any thing...an Uncle of mine was present...and...one of the Monks, his Friend, told him that every one of the Convent had given to him his Cell...wherein was...his Bed and Apparell, which was but simple and of small Price. Which Monk willed my Uncle to buy something of him; who said, I see nothing that is worth Money to my use: No, said he; give me iid(two pence) for my Cell Door, which was never made with vs(five shillings). No, said my Uncle, I know not what to do with it (for he was a Young Man unmarried, and then neither stood need of Houses nor Doors). But such Persons as afterward brought their Corn or Hay or suchlike, found all the doors either open or the Locks and Shackles plucked away, or the Door itself taken away, went in and took what they found, filched it away...the Church was the first thing that was put to the spoil; and then the Abbot's Lodging, Dortor, and Frater, with the Cloister and all the Buildings thereabout...for nothing was spared but the Ox-houses and swinecoates...which had more favour shewed them than the very Church itself. It would have pitied any Heart to see what tearing up of the Lead there was, and plucking up of Boards, and throwing down of the Sparres...and the Tombs in the Church all broken...and all things of Price, either spoiled, carped(plucked) away or defaced to the uttermost.

The persons that cast the Lead into foders (1 fother = 1 ton approx.) pluck'd up all the Seats in the Choir...and burned them, and melted the Lead therewithall: although there was wood in plenty within a flight shot of them...For the better Proof of this my Saying, I demanded of my Father, thirty years after the Suppression, which had bought part of the Timber of the Church, and all the Timber of the Steeple, with the Bell Frame, with others his partners therein...whether he thought well of the Religious Persons and of the Religion then used? And he told me Yea: for said He, I did see no Cause to the contrary: Well, said I, then how came it to pass you was so ready to destroy and spoil the thing that you thought well of? What should I do, said He; might I not as well as others have some Profit of the Spoil of the Abbey? For I did see all would away; and therefore I did as others did.

Michael Sherbrook 'The Fall of Religious Houses, 1567-1591'

Although Sherbrook's story accords with both the archaeological evidence and what we know from other sites, the Roche monks were treated quite well. The brethren received 20s each towards new clothing and half of their agreed annual pensions in advance. The abbot retained his books, plate and household goods, a chalice, a vestment and £30 in cash.

Typical contents

The Churche.- An alter of woode paynted at the hyghe alter; iiij candlestykes of brasse and ij litell candelstykes; the deskes in the church; the Chapell of Saynt Michell, new made by the abbott; iiij lytel alters in the Chapell of St. Anne; a lytell payre of organes; an alter in our Lady Chapell and ij images, a partycon and seates of oke; the pavements in our Lady Chapell; a payr of organs in our Lady Chapell; the pavyng in the body of the church; in the body of the church ij alters inclosyd with oke; the rood-lofte. . . . . lxs.

The Kechynne. -vj brasse pottes; iiij pannes; iii spyttes; j fryeng panne; j payr of rostyng ieronnes; j barre to hang potts on; iij potthokes; j morter of brasse; sould to Mr. Willm. Cavendysh, Esquier, for. . . . xl s..

Inventory for Lilleshall Abbey, Shropshire, at the Dissolution. (Extract)

BIBLIOGRAPHY AND RESOURCES

BIBLIOGRAPHY

General Reference

Bottomley, F, **The Abbey Explorer's Guide**, Kaye and Ward, 1981, ISBN 0-7182-1280-0. Very useful; full glossary and brief gazeteer.

Butler, L and Given-Wilson, C, **Medieval Monasteries of Great Britain,** Michael Joseph, 1979, ISBN 0-7181-1614-3.Informative introduction and gazeteer.

Clark, J W, **The Book of Observances according to the Rule of S. Augustine,** Macmillan and Bowes, Cambridge, 1897. Authentic detail about Barnwell Priory, Cambridgeshire.

Coppack, G, **English Heritage Book of Abbeys and Priories**, Batsford, 1990, ISBN 0-7134-6308-2. Archaeological analysis especially useful on sanitation, the Suppression and building conversions.

Dugdale, Sir W, **Monasticon Anglicanum,** 6 vols, 1817-30. Massive compendium, incorporating documents.

Gilyard-Beer, R, **Abbeys**, HMSO, 1976, ISBN 0-11-670776-3. Succinct academic overview.

Knowles, Dom D, **The Monastic Order in England,** 1963, Cambridge University Press. ISBN 0-521-05479-6. Classic work by the acknowledged authority covering both history and institutions.

Knowles, Dom D, **The Religious Orders in England**, 3 vols, Cambridge University Press, 1979, ISBN 0-521-29566-1. The great standard work.

Knowles, Dom D and Hadcock, R N, **Medieval Religious Houses: England and Wales**, 1971, Longman, ISBN 0-582-112-30-3. Historical introduction and statistical gazeteer.

Little, B, **Abbeys and Priories in England and Wales**, Batsford, 1979, ISBN 0-7134-1712-9. Gazeteer and survey, including modern communities.

Parry, D, (trans) **The Rule of Saint Benedict**, Darton, Longman and Todd, 1984, ISBN 0-232-51584. The essential text.

Power, E, **Medieval English Nunneries**, 1922, Cambridge. Interesting details of individual nuns in specific monasteries.

Platt, C P S, **The Abbeys and Priories of Medieval England**, Secker and Warburg, 1984, ISBN 0-436-37557-5. Readable and scholarly account.

Platt, C, **Abbeys of Yorkshire,** English Heritage, 1988, ISBN 1-85074-199-9. Highly illustrated and easy to read.

Victoria History of the Counties Series. Vol 2 always covers abbeys.

Wright, G N, **Discovering Abbeys and Priories**, Shire Publications, 1969, ISBN 0-85263-454-4. Concise pocket guide.

Youings, J, **The Dissolution of the Monasteries,** Allen and Unwin, 1971, ISBN 0-04-942089-5. Detailed introduction and collection of primary sources.

Building

Harvey, J H, **Mediaeval Craftsmen**, Batsford, 1975, ISBN 0-7134-2934-8. Analyses the crafts and their respective skills and incorporates medieval manuscript illustrations.

Salzman, L F, **Building in England down to 1540**, Clarendon Press, 1952, ISBN 0-19-817158-7 Interesting and informative.

Sorrell, M, (ed.), **Alan Sorrell Reconstructing the Past**, Batsford, 1981, ISBN 0-713-4158-8. Reconstuction drawings, including abbeys.

Tiles

Eames, E, **English Medieval Tiles**, British Museum, 1985, ISBN 0-7141-2029-4. Clear text with beautiful illustrations.

Greene, J P, Johnston, B, Noake, and Bearpark, P, **Medieval Floor Tiles: How they were made,** Norton Priory Museum, 1979. Concise text, aptly illustrated.

Food

Black, M, **Medieval Food and Cooking**, English Heritage, 1985, ISBN 1-85074-081-X. Resumé plus medieval recipes, helpfully adapted.

Peplow, E and Peplow, R, **In a Monastery Garden**, David and Charles, 1988, ISBN 0-7153-8966-1.

Teaching strategies

Anderson, C, 'A Recipe for the Past', **Remnants**, 3, pp 17-19, 1986. How to run a Living History event.

Archaeological Detectives Poster Games. Four posters. Available from English Heritage postal sales.

Aston, O, **Primary History Problem Solving**, Shropshire Education Department, 1989. Problem-solving techniques on historic sites, including abbeys.

Brittain, P, 'Get the Abbey Habit', **Remnants**, 1, pp 2-4, 1986. A term's work for primary pupils from their abbey visit.

Corbishley, M, 'Not much to look at', **Remnants**, 1, pp 1-2, 1986. First steps in the hunt for evidence.

Corbishley, M, 'The case of the blocked window', **Remnants**, 2, pp 1-4, 1986. Using stratigraphy to understand a building.

Corbishley, M, 'Miss...please miss, why did people live underground?', **Remnants**, 3, pp 1-3, 1987. Drawing conclusions from archaeological remains.

Corbishley, M, 'Coping with the bird's eye view', **Remnants**, 4, pp 5-7, 1987. Helping children to understand plans.

Fairclough, J and Redsell, P, **Living History: reconstructing the past with children,** English Heritage, 1985, ISBN 1-85074-073-9. Good practice in Suffolk.

Goodhew, E (ed), **'Museums and**

Primary Science', Area Museums Service for South Eastern England, 1989, ISBN 0-90-4752-06-2. Classwork ideas applicable to sites.

Knight, J, 'En route...Thornton Abbey', **Remnants**, 11, pp 3-6, 1990. Cross-curricular work in model-making and re-enactment.

Case studies

Cann, J and Bartholomew, J, **Cathedrals**, distributed by Fernleaf Educational Software, Cross-curricular approaches; particularly detailed on science.

Clark, M (words) and Young, L (music), **Blackfriars**, Newcastle Architecture Workshop, 1985. A song cycle based on the history of the friary.

Durham County Joint Curriculum Study Group, **Craftsmen for Christ**. Copies may be purchased from the Dean and Chapter Library, The Cathedral, Durham. Useful on building methods and preservation techniques.

Morris, R, **Bare Ruined Choirs**, Stanley Thornes, 1987, ISBN 0-85950-544-8. Thoroughly-documented account of the Dissolution of Vale Crucis Abbey.

Scoffham, S, **St Augustine's Abbey**, Canterbury, English Heritage, 1988, ISBN 1-85074-196-4. Handbook of suggestions for teachers, including copyright-free class sheets and trail sheets.

Ward, E, Mulligan, F and Aspley, M, **Inch Abbey**, Q.U.B. Teachers' Centre, 1985, ISBN 0-85389-257-1. Site-based study of an early Celtic and a later Cistercian abbey.

Watling, S, **Cleeve and Muchelney Abbeys**, English Heritage, 1989, ISBN 1-85074-238-3. Handbook of suggestions for teachers, including copyright-free information sheets and activity sheets.

A Search in Evidence: Nendrum, South Eastern Education and Library Board NICED. Obtainable from the Learning Resources Unit, Stranmillis College, Belfast BT9 5DY. An evidence-based study of an early monastery.

Children's Books

Boyd, A, **Life in a Medieval Monastery**, Introduction to World History Series, Cambridge University Press, 1987, ISBN 0-521-33724-0.

Caselli, G, **The Everyday Life of a Medieval Monk**, Macdonald, 1986, ISBN 0-356-11370-1.

Leyser, H, **Medieval Women**, Presenting the Past Topics, pp 8-11, Oxford University Press, 1988, ISBN 0-19-913347-6.

Macaulay, D, **Cathedral: The Story of Its Construction**, Collins, 1988, ISBN 0-00-192160-6.

Pluckrose, H, **Monasteries and Cathedrals**, On Location Series, Mills and Boon, 1975, ISBN 0-263-05990-1.

Reeves, M, **The Medieval Monastery**, Then and There Series, Longman, 1988, ISBN 0-582-00380-6.

Rutland, J, **See inside an Abbey**, Hutchinson, 1978, ISBN 0-091-28680-8.

Sauvain, P, **An Abbey**, Imagining the Past Series, Macmillan Education, 1976, ISBN 0-333-15209-3.

Scarfe, N, **A Monk named Jocelyn**: Life in an Abbey in Medieval England, Chambers, 1976, ISBN 0-550-75521-7.

Sayers, J, **Life in the Medieval Monastery**, Focus on History Series, Longman, 1969, ISBN 0-552-18238-7.

Watson, P, **Building the Medieval Cathedrals**, Cambridge University Press, 1976, ISBN 0-52108-711-2.

Fiction

Andrews, J S, **The Bell of Nendrum**, Blackstaff, 1985, ISBN 0-85640-341-5.

Lively, P, **Boy without a Name**, Heinemann, 1975, ISBN 0-434-94916-7.

Sutcliff, R, **The Witch's Brat**, Oxford University Press, 1970, ISBN 0-19-271321-3.

VISUAL AIDS

Videos

The Archaeological Detectives, English Heritage,1990. For age 9-13; 20 minutes. Available from English Heritage postal sales: PO Box 229, Northampton NN6 9RY

Clues Challenge, English Heritage, 1990. For age 9-13; 20 minutes. Available from English Heritage postal sales.

The Mystery, English Heritage, 1990. For age 9-13; 20 minutes. Available from English Heritage postal sales.

Building an Abbey: Rievaulx, English Heritage, 1988, For age 9-13; 14 minutes. Available from English Heritage postal sales.

Living History, English Heritage, 1986, Teachers; 21 minutes. Available from English Heritage postal sales.

Looking at an Abbey, English Heritage, 1980, For age 11-13; 17 minutes. Available from English Heritage postal sales.

Gerald of Wales, CADW, 9th Floor, Brunel House, 2 Fitzalan Road , Cardiff CF2 1UY together with **'Gerald meets the Monks'**, a booklet available for primary pupils, 1988, 25 minutes.

Grey Abbey, Learning Resources Unit, Stranmillis College, Belfast BT9 5DY. 22 minutes.

The Master Builders: the construction of a great church, English Heritage, 1991. For age 14 upwards. 23 minutes. Available from English Heritage postal sales.

Buildings and Beliefs, English Heritage, 1990. For age 14 upwards. 20 minutes. Available from English Heritage postal sales.

ENGLISH HERITAGE

Seal of Roche Abbey

Acknowledgements

My grateful thanks are offered to Oliver Aston, Stephen Scoffham and Sue Watling for many ideas incorporated in the text; to Beric Morley and Bob Morris for advice and encouragement; to Patricia Brittain and the staff and pupils of St Andrews C. E. Primary School, Nesscliffe, Shropshire and John Knight and the staff and pupils of East Halton Junior and Infant School, South Humberside for their work in school and on site.